FOREX TRADING

JOURNAL

Printed by CreateSpace, An Amazon.com Company

This forex trading journal or logbook is designed by a forex trader. Unlike other forex trading journals, it contains pages to record trading of currency pairs as well as pages to record your trading strategies. To allow easy reference of recorded trading strategies, it has an Index Section for you to record the page numbers so you can find your strategies easily.

There are 2 sections in this journal.

Section 1: Recording of individual trades - Record up to 400 Trades

Section 2: Record The Trade Setup of Your FX Trading Strategies - Record Up to 50 Trading Strategies Setup Info

SAMPLE PAGES

Date:		Time Open:		Time Closed:		
Currency Pair	Buy / Sell	Trade Size	Entry Price	Target Price	Stop Loss	Closing Price
Profit /Loss (Pips):		Strategy:		Notes:		

Date:		Time Open:		Time Closed:		
Currency Pair	Buy / Sell	Trade Size	Entry Price	Target Price	Stop Loss	Closing Price
Profit /Loss (Pips):		Strategy:		Notes:		

Date:		Time Open:		Time Closed:		
Currency Pair	Buy / Sell	Trade Size	Entry Price	Target Price	Stop Loss	Closing Price
Profit /Loss (Pips):		Strategy:		Notes:		

Date:		Time Open:		Time Closed:		
Currency Pair	Buy / Sell	Trade Size	Entry Price	Target Price	Stop Loss	Closing Price
Profit /Loss (Pips):		Strategy:		Notes:		

Date:		Time Open:		Time Closed:		
Currency Pair	Buy / Sell	Trade Size	Entry Price	Target Price	Stop Loss	Closing Price
Profit /Loss (Pips):		Strategy:		Notes:		

5

Trading Strategy Name:	Currency Pair:

Indicators Used	
Buy Signal	
Sell Signal	
Profit Target	
Stop Loss	
Notes	

87

Date:		Time Open:		Time Closed:		
Currency Pair	Buy / Sell	Trade Size	Entry Price	Target Price	Stop Loss	Closing Price
Profit /Loss (Pips):		Strategy:		Notes:		

Date:		Time Open:		Time Closed:		
Currency Pair	Buy / Sell	Trade Size	Entry Price	Target Price	Stop Loss	Closing Price
Profit /Loss (Pips):		Strategy:		Notes:		

Date:		Time Open:		Time Closed:		
Currency Pair	Buy / Sell	Trade Size	Entry Price	Target Price	Stop Loss	Closing Price
Profit /Loss (Pips):		Strategy:		Notes:		

Date:		Time Open:		Time Closed:		
Currency Pair	Buy / Sell	Trade Size	Entry Price	Target Price	Stop Loss	Closing Price
Profit /Loss (Pips):		Strategy:		Notes:		

Date:		Time Open:		Time Closed:		
Currency Pair	Buy / Sell	Trade Size	Entry Price	Target Price	Stop Loss	Closing Price
Profit /Loss (Pips):		Strategy:		Notes:		

Date:		Time Open:		Time Closed:		
Currency Pair	Buy / Sell	Trade Size	Entry Price	Target Price	Stop Loss	Closing Price
Profit /Loss (Pips):		Strategy:		Notes:		

Date:		Time Open:		Time Closed:		
Currency Pair	Buy / Sell	Trade Size	Entry Price	Target Price	Stop Loss	Closing Price
Profit /Loss (Pips):		Strategy:		Notes:		

Date:		Time Open:		Time Closed:		
Currency Pair	Buy / Sell	Trade Size	Entry Price	Target Price	Stop Loss	Closing Price
Profit /Loss (Pips):		Strategy:		Notes:		

Date:		Time Open:		Time Closed:		
Currency Pair	Buy / Sell	Trade Size	Entry Price	Target Price	Stop Loss	Closing Price
Profit /Loss (Pips):		Strategy:		Notes:		

Date:		Time Open:		Time Closed:		
Currency Pair	Buy / Sell	Trade Size	Entry Price	Target Price	Stop Loss	Closing Price
Profit /Loss (Pips):		Strategy:		Notes:		

Date:		Time Open:		Time Closed:		
Currency Pair	**Buy / Sell**	**Trade Size**	**Entry Price**	**Target Price**	**Stop Loss**	**Closing Price**
Profit /Loss (Pips):		Strategy:		Notes:		

Date:		Time Open:		Time Closed:		
Currency Pair	**Buy / Sell**	**Trade Size**	**Entry Price**	**Target Price**	**Stop Loss**	**Closing Price**
Profit /Loss (Pips):		Strategy:		Notes:		

Date:		Time Open:		Time Closed:		
Currency Pair	**Buy / Sell**	**Trade Size**	**Entry Price**	**Target Price**	**Stop Loss**	**Closing Price**
Profit /Loss (Pips):		Strategy:		Notes:		

Date:		Time Open:		Time Closed:		
Currency Pair	**Buy / Sell**	**Trade Size**	**Entry Price**	**Target Price**	**Stop Loss**	**Closing Price**
Profit /Loss (Pips):		Strategy:		Notes:		

Date:		Time Open:		Time Closed:		
Currency Pair	**Buy / Sell**	**Trade Size**	**Entry Price**	**Target Price**	**Stop Loss**	**Closing Price**
Profit /Loss (Pips):		Strategy:		Notes:		

Date:		Time Open:		Time Closed:		
Currency Pair	Buy / Sell	Trade Size	Entry Price	Target Price	Stop Loss	Closing Price
Profit /Loss (Pips):		Strategy:		Notes:		

Date:		Time Open:		Time Closed:		
Currency Pair	Buy / Sell	Trade Size	Entry Price	Target Price	Stop Loss	Closing Price
Profit /Loss (Pips):		Strategy:		Notes:		

Date:		Time Open:		Time Closed:		
Currency Pair	Buy / Sell	Trade Size	Entry Price	Target Price	Stop Loss	Closing Price
Profit /Loss (Pips):		Strategy:		Notes:		

Date:		Time Open:		Time Closed:		
Currency Pair	Buy / Sell	Trade Size	Entry Price	Target Price	Stop Loss	Closing Price
Profit /Loss (Pips):		Strategy:		Notes:		

Date:		Time Open:		Time Closed:		
Currency Pair	Buy / Sell	Trade Size	Entry Price	Target Price	Stop Loss	Closing Price
Profit /Loss (Pips):		Strategy:		Notes:		

Date:		Time Open:		Time Closed:		
Currency Pair	Buy / Sell	Trade Size	Entry Price	Target Price	Stop Loss	Closing Price
Profit /Loss (Pips):		Strategy:		Notes:		

Date:		Time Open:		Time Closed:		
Currency Pair	Buy / Sell	Trade Size	Entry Price	Target Price	Stop Loss	Closing Price
Profit /Loss (Pips):		Strategy:		Notes:		

Date:		Time Open:		Time Closed:		
Currency Pair	Buy / Sell	Trade Size	Entry Price	Target Price	Stop Loss	Closing Price
Profit /Loss (Pips):		Strategy:		Notes:		

Date:		Time Open:		Time Closed:		
Currency Pair	Buy / Sell	Trade Size	Entry Price	Target Price	Stop Loss	Closing Price
Profit /Loss (Pips):		Strategy:		Notes:		

Date:		Time Open:		Time Closed:		
Currency Pair	Buy / Sell	Trade Size	Entry Price	Target Price	Stop Loss	Closing Price
Profit /Loss (Pips):		Strategy:		Notes:		

Date:		Time Open:		Time Closed:		
Currency Pair	Buy / Sell	Trade Size	Entry Price	Target Price	Stop Loss	Closing Price
Profit /Loss (Pips):		Strategy:		Notes:		

Date:		Time Open:		Time Closed:		
Currency Pair	Buy / Sell	Trade Size	Entry Price	Target Price	Stop Loss	Closing Price
Profit /Loss (Pips):		Strategy:		Notes:		

Date:		Time Open:		Time Closed:		
Currency Pair	Buy / Sell	Trade Size	Entry Price	Target Price	Stop Loss	Closing Price
Profit /Loss (Pips):		Strategy:		Notes:		

Date:		Time Open:		Time Closed:		
Currency Pair	Buy / Sell	Trade Size	Entry Price	Target Price	Stop Loss	Closing Price
Profit /Loss (Pips):		Strategy:		Notes:		

Date:		Time Open:		Time Closed:		
Currency Pair	Buy / Sell	Trade Size	Entry Price	Target Price	Stop Loss	Closing Price
Profit /Loss (Pips):		Strategy:		Notes:		

Date:		Time Open:		Time Closed:		
Currency Pair	**Buy / Sell**	**Trade Size**	**Entry Price**	**Target Price**	**Stop Loss**	**Closing Price**
Profit /Loss (Pips):		Strategy:		Notes:		

Date:		Time Open:		Time Closed:		
Currency Pair	**Buy / Sell**	**Trade Size**	**Entry Price**	**Target Price**	**Stop Loss**	**Closing Price**
Profit /Loss (Pips):		Strategy:		Notes:		

Date:		Time Open:		Time Closed:		
Currency Pair	**Buy / Sell**	**Trade Size**	**Entry Price**	**Target Price**	**Stop Loss**	**Closing Price**
Profit /Loss (Pips):		Strategy:		Notes:		

Date:		Time Open:		Time Closed:		
Currency Pair	**Buy / Sell**	**Trade Size**	**Entry Price**	**Target Price**	**Stop Loss**	**Closing Price**
Profit /Loss (Pips):		Strategy:		Notes:		

Date:		Time Open:		Time Closed:		
Currency Pair	**Buy / Sell**	**Trade Size**	**Entry Price**	**Target Price**	**Stop Loss**	**Closing Price**
Profit /Loss (Pips):		Strategy:		Notes:		

Date:		Time Open:		Time Closed:		
Currency Pair	Buy / Sell	Trade Size	Entry Price	Target Price	Stop Loss	Closing Price
Profit /Loss (Pips):		Strategy:		Notes:		

Date:		Time Open:		Time Closed:		
Currency Pair	Buy / Sell	Trade Size	Entry Price	Target Price	Stop Loss	Closing Price
Profit /Loss (Pips):		Strategy:		Notes:		

Date:		Time Open:		Time Closed:		
Currency Pair	Buy / Sell	Trade Size	Entry Price	Target Price	Stop Loss	Closing Price
Profit /Loss (Pips):		Strategy:		Notes:		

Date:		Time Open:		Time Closed:		
Currency Pair	Buy / Sell	Trade Size	Entry Price	Target Price	Stop Loss	Closing Price
Profit /Loss (Pips):		Strategy:		Notes:		

Date:		Time Open:		Time Closed:		
Currency Pair	Buy / Sell	Trade Size	Entry Price	Target Price	Stop Loss	Closing Price
Profit /Loss (Pips):		Strategy:		Notes:		

Date:		Time Open:		Time Closed:		
Currency Pair	Buy / Sell	Trade Size	Entry Price	Target Price	Stop Loss	Closing Price
Profit /Loss (Pips):		Strategy:		Notes:		

Date:		Time Open:		Time Closed:		
Currency Pair	Buy / Sell	Trade Size	Entry Price	Target Price	Stop Loss	Closing Price
Profit /Loss (Pips):		Strategy:		Notes:		

Date:		Time Open:		Time Closed:		
Currency Pair	Buy / Sell	Trade Size	Entry Price	Target Price	Stop Loss	Closing Price
Profit /Loss (Pips):		Strategy:		Notes:		

Date:		Time Open:		Time Closed:		
Currency Pair	Buy / Sell	Trade Size	Entry Price	Target Price	Stop Loss	Closing Price
Profit /Loss (Pips):		Strategy:		Notes:		

Date:		Time Open:		Time Closed:		
Currency Pair	Buy / Sell	Trade Size	Entry Price	Target Price	Stop Loss	Closing Price
Profit /Loss (Pips):		Strategy:		Notes:		

Date:		Time Open:		Time Closed:		
Currency Pair	Buy / Sell	Trade Size	Entry Price	Target Price	Stop Loss	Closing Price
Profit /Loss (Pips):		Strategy:		Notes:		

Date:		Time Open:		Time Closed:		
Currency Pair	Buy / Sell	Trade Size	Entry Price	Target Price	Stop Loss	Closing Price
Profit /Loss (Pips):		Strategy:		Notes:		

Date:		Time Open:		Time Closed:		
Currency Pair	Buy / Sell	Trade Size	Entry Price	Target Price	Stop Loss	Closing Price
Profit /Loss (Pips):		Strategy:		Notes:		

Date:		Time Open:		Time Closed:		
Currency Pair	Buy / Sell	Trade Size	Entry Price	Target Price	Stop Loss	Closing Price
Profit /Loss (Pips):		Strategy:		Notes:		

Date:		Time Open:		Time Closed:		
Currency Pair	Buy / Sell	Trade Size	Entry Price	Target Price	Stop Loss	Closing Price
Profit /Loss (Pips):		Strategy:		Notes:		

Date:		Time Open:		Time Closed:		
Currency Pair	Buy / Sell	Trade Size	Entry Price	Target Price	Stop Loss	Closing Price
Profit /Loss (Pips):		Strategy:		Notes:		

Date:		Time Open:		Time Closed:		
Currency Pair	Buy / Sell	Trade Size	Entry Price	Target Price	Stop Loss	Closing Price
Profit /Loss (Pips):		Strategy:		Notes:		

Date:		Time Open:		Time Closed:		
Currency Pair	Buy / Sell	Trade Size	Entry Price	Target Price	Stop Loss	Closing Price
Profit /Loss (Pips):		Strategy:		Notes:		

Date:		Time Open:		Time Closed:		
Currency Pair	Buy / Sell	Trade Size	Entry Price	Target Price	Stop Loss	Closing Price
Profit /Loss (Pips):		Strategy:		Notes:		

Date:		Time Open:		Time Closed:		
Currency Pair	Buy / Sell	Trade Size	Entry Price	Target Price	Stop Loss	Closing Price
Profit /Loss (Pips):		Strategy:		Notes:		

Date:		Time Open:		Time Closed:		
Currency Pair	Buy / Sell	Trade Size	Entry Price	Target Price	Stop Loss	Closing Price
Profit /Loss (Pips):		Strategy:		Notes:		

Date:		Time Open:		Time Closed:		
Currency Pair	Buy / Sell	Trade Size	Entry Price	Target Price	Stop Loss	Closing Price
Profit /Loss (Pips):		Strategy:		Notes:		

Date:		Time Open:		Time Closed:		
Currency Pair	Buy / Sell	Trade Size	Entry Price	Target Price	Stop Loss	Closing Price
Profit /Loss (Pips):		Strategy:		Notes:		

Date:		Time Open:		Time Closed:		
Currency Pair	Buy / Sell	Trade Size	Entry Price	Target Price	Stop Loss	Closing Price
Profit /Loss (Pips):		Strategy:		Notes:		

Date:		Time Open:		Time Closed:		
Currency Pair	Buy / Sell	Trade Size	Entry Price	Target Price	Stop Loss	Closing Price
Profit /Loss (Pips):		Strategy:		Notes:		

Date:		Time Open:		Time Closed:		
Currency Pair	**Buy / Sell**	**Trade Size**	**Entry Price**	**Target Price**	**Stop Loss**	**Closing Price**
Profit /Loss (Pips):		Strategy:		Notes:		

Date:		Time Open:		Time Closed:		
Currency Pair	**Buy / Sell**	**Trade Size**	**Entry Price**	**Target Price**	**Stop Loss**	**Closing Price**
Profit /Loss (Pips):		Strategy:		Notes:		

Date:		Time Open:		Time Closed:		
Currency Pair	**Buy / Sell**	**Trade Size**	**Entry Price**	**Target Price**	**Stop Loss**	**Closing Price**
Profit /Loss (Pips):		Strategy:		Notes:		

Date:		Time Open:		Time Closed:		
Currency Pair	**Buy / Sell**	**Trade Size**	**Entry Price**	**Target Price**	**Stop Loss**	**Closing Price**
Profit /Loss (Pips):		Strategy:		Notes:		

Date:		Time Open:		Time Closed:		
Currency Pair	**Buy / Sell**	**Trade Size**	**Entry Price**	**Target Price**	**Stop Loss**	**Closing Price**
Profit /Loss (Pips):		Strategy:		Notes:		

Date:		Time Open:		Time Closed:		
Currency Pair	Buy / Sell	Trade Size	Entry Price	Target Price	Stop Loss	Closing Price
Profit /Loss (Pips):		Strategy:		Notes:		

Date:		Time Open:		Time Closed:		
Currency Pair	Buy / Sell	Trade Size	Entry Price	Target Price	Stop Loss	Closing Price
Profit /Loss (Pips):		Strategy:		Notes:		

Date:		Time Open:		Time Closed:		
Currency Pair	Buy / Sell	Trade Size	Entry Price	Target Price	Stop Loss	Closing Price
Profit /Loss (Pips):		Strategy:		Notes:		

Date:		Time Open:		Time Closed:		
Currency Pair	Buy / Sell	Trade Size	Entry Price	Target Price	Stop Loss	Closing Price
Profit /Loss (Pips):		Strategy:		Notes:		

Date:		Time Open:		Time Closed:		
Currency Pair	Buy / Sell	Trade Size	Entry Price	Target Price	Stop Loss	Closing Price
Profit /Loss (Pips):		Strategy:		Notes:		

Date:		Time Open:		Time Closed:		
Currency Pair	**Buy / Sell**	**Trade Size**	**Entry Price**	**Target Price**	**Stop Loss**	**Closing Price**
Profit /Loss (Pips):		Strategy:		Notes:		

Date:		Time Open:		Time Closed:		
Currency Pair	**Buy / Sell**	**Trade Size**	**Entry Price**	**Target Price**	**Stop Loss**	**Closing Price**
Profit /Loss (Pips):		Strategy:		Notes:		

Date:		Time Open:		Time Closed:		
Currency Pair	**Buy / Sell**	**Trade Size**	**Entry Price**	**Target Price**	**Stop Loss**	**Closing Price**
Profit /Loss (Pips):		Strategy:		Notes:		

Date:		Time Open:		Time Closed:		
Currency Pair	**Buy / Sell**	**Trade Size**	**Entry Price**	**Target Price**	**Stop Loss**	**Closing Price**
Profit /Loss (Pips):		Strategy:		Notes:		

Date:		Time Open:		Time Closed:		
Currency Pair	**Buy / Sell**	**Trade Size**	**Entry Price**	**Target Price**	**Stop Loss**	**Closing Price**
Profit /Loss (Pips):		Strategy:		Notes:		

Date:		Time Open:		Time Closed:		
Currency Pair	Buy / Sell	Trade Size	Entry Price	Target Price	Stop Loss	Closing Price
Profit /Loss (Pips):		Strategy:		Notes:		

Date:		Time Open:		Time Closed:		
Currency Pair	Buy / Sell	Trade Size	Entry Price	Target Price	Stop Loss	Closing Price
Profit /Loss (Pips):		Strategy:		Notes:		

Date:		Time Open:		Time Closed:		
Currency Pair	Buy / Sell	Trade Size	Entry Price	Target Price	Stop Loss	Closing Price
Profit /Loss (Pips):		Strategy:		Notes:		

Date:		Time Open:		Time Closed:		
Currency Pair	Buy / Sell	Trade Size	Entry Price	Target Price	Stop Loss	Closing Price
Profit /Loss (Pips):		Strategy:		Notes:		

Date:		Time Open:		Time Closed:		
Currency Pair	Buy / Sell	Trade Size	Entry Price	Target Price	Stop Loss	Closing Price
Profit /Loss (Pips):		Strategy:		Notes:		

Date:		Time Open:		Time Closed:		
Currency Pair	Buy / Sell	Trade Size	Entry Price	Target Price	Stop Loss	Closing Price
Profit /Loss (Pips):		Strategy:		Notes:		

Date:		Time Open:		Time Closed:		
Currency Pair	Buy / Sell	Trade Size	Entry Price	Target Price	Stop Loss	Closing Price
Profit /Loss (Pips):		Strategy:		Notes:		

Date:		Time Open:		Time Closed:		
Currency Pair	Buy / Sell	Trade Size	Entry Price	Target Price	Stop Loss	Closing Price
Profit /Loss (Pips):		Strategy:		Notes:		

Date:		Time Open:		Time Closed:		
Currency Pair	Buy / Sell	Trade Size	Entry Price	Target Price	Stop Loss	Closing Price
Profit /Loss (Pips):		Strategy:		Notes:		

Date:		Time Open:		Time Closed:		
Currency Pair	Buy / Sell	Trade Size	Entry Price	Target Price	Stop Loss	Closing Price
Profit /Loss (Pips):		Strategy:		Notes:		

Date:		Time Open:		Time Closed:		
Currency Pair	Buy / Sell	Trade Size	Entry Price	Target Price	Stop Loss	Closing Price
Profit /Loss (Pips):		Strategy:		Notes:		

Date:		Time Open:		Time Closed:		
Currency Pair	Buy / Sell	Trade Size	Entry Price	Target Price	Stop Loss	Closing Price
Profit /Loss (Pips):		Strategy:		Notes:		

Date:		Time Open:		Time Closed:		
Currency Pair	Buy / Sell	Trade Size	Entry Price	Target Price	Stop Loss	Closing Price
Profit /Loss (Pips):		Strategy:		Notes:		

Date:		Time Open:		Time Closed:		
Currency Pair	Buy / Sell	Trade Size	Entry Price	Target Price	Stop Loss	Closing Price
Profit /Loss (Pips):		Strategy:		Notes:		

Date:		Time Open:		Time Closed:		
Currency Pair	Buy / Sell	Trade Size	Entry Price	Target Price	Stop Loss	Closing Price
Profit /Loss (Pips):		Strategy:		Notes:		

Date:		Time Open:		Time Closed:		
Currency Pair	Buy / Sell	Trade Size	Entry Price	Target Price	Stop Loss	Closing Price
Profit /Loss (Pips):		Strategy:		Notes:		

Date:		Time Open:		Time Closed:		
Currency Pair	Buy / Sell	Trade Size	Entry Price	Target Price	Stop Loss	Closing Price
Profit /Loss (Pips):		Strategy:		Notes:		

Date:		Time Open:		Time Closed:		
Currency Pair	Buy / Sell	Trade Size	Entry Price	Target Price	Stop Loss	Closing Price
Profit /Loss (Pips):		Strategy:		Notes:		

Date:		Time Open:		Time Closed:		
Currency Pair	Buy / Sell	Trade Size	Entry Price	Target Price	Stop Loss	Closing Price
Profit /Loss (Pips):		Strategy:		Notes:		

Date:		Time Open:		Time Closed:		
Currency Pair	Buy / Sell	Trade Size	Entry Price	Target Price	Stop Loss	Closing Price
Profit /Loss (Pips):		Strategy:		Notes:		

Date:		Time Open:		Time Closed:		
Currency Pair	Buy / Sell	Trade Size	Entry Price	Target Price	Stop Loss	Closing Price
Profit /Loss (Pips):		Strategy:		Notes:		

Date:		Time Open:		Time Closed:		
Currency Pair	Buy / Sell	Trade Size	Entry Price	Target Price	Stop Loss	Closing Price
Profit /Loss (Pips):		Strategy:		Notes:		

Date:		Time Open:		Time Closed:		
Currency Pair	Buy / Sell	Trade Size	Entry Price	Target Price	Stop Loss	Closing Price
Profit /Loss (Pips):		Strategy:		Notes:		

Date:		Time Open:		Time Closed:		
Currency Pair	Buy / Sell	Trade Size	Entry Price	Target Price	Stop Loss	Closing Price
Profit /Loss (Pips):		Strategy:		Notes:		

Date:		Time Open:		Time Closed:		
Currency Pair	Buy / Sell	Trade Size	Entry Price	Target Price	Stop Loss	Closing Price
Profit /Loss (Pips):		Strategy:		Notes:		

Date:		Time Open:		Time Closed:		
Currency Pair	Buy / Sell	Trade Size	Entry Price	Target Price	Stop Loss	Closing Price
Profit /Loss (Pips):		Strategy:		Notes:		

Date:		Time Open:		Time Closed:		
Currency Pair	Buy / Sell	Trade Size	Entry Price	Target Price	Stop Loss	Closing Price
Profit /Loss (Pips):		Strategy:		Notes:		

Date:		Time Open:		Time Closed:		
Currency Pair	Buy / Sell	Trade Size	Entry Price	Target Price	Stop Loss	Closing Price
Profit /Loss (Pips):		Strategy:		Notes:		

Date:		Time Open:		Time Closed:		
Currency Pair	Buy / Sell	Trade Size	Entry Price	Target Price	Stop Loss	Closing Price
Profit /Loss (Pips):		Strategy:		Notes:		

Date:		Time Open:		Time Closed:		
Currency Pair	Buy / Sell	Trade Size	Entry Price	Target Price	Stop Loss	Closing Price
Profit /Loss (Pips):		Strategy:		Notes:		

Date:		Time Open:		Time Closed:		
Currency Pair	Buy / Sell	Trade Size	Entry Price	Target Price	Stop Loss	Closing Price
Profit /Loss (Pips):		Strategy:		Notes:		

Date:		Time Open:		Time Closed:		
Currency Pair	Buy / Sell	Trade Size	Entry Price	Target Price	Stop Loss	Closing Price
Profit /Loss (Pips):		Strategy:		Notes:		

Date:		Time Open:		Time Closed:		
Currency Pair	Buy / Sell	Trade Size	Entry Price	Target Price	Stop Loss	Closing Price
Profit /Loss (Pips):		Strategy:		Notes:		

Date:		Time Open:		Time Closed:		
Currency Pair	Buy / Sell	Trade Size	Entry Price	Target Price	Stop Loss	Closing Price
Profit /Loss (Pips):		Strategy:		Notes:		

Date:		Time Open:		Time Closed:		
Currency Pair	Buy / Sell	Trade Size	Entry Price	Target Price	Stop Loss	Closing Price
Profit /Loss (Pips):		Strategy:		Notes:		

Date:		Time Open:		Time Closed:		
Currency Pair	Buy / Sell	Trade Size	Entry Price	Target Price	Stop Loss	Closing Price
Profit /Loss (Pips):		Strategy:		Notes:		

Date:		Time Open:		Time Closed:		
Currency Pair	Buy / Sell	Trade Size	Entry Price	Target Price	Stop Loss	Closing Price
Profit /Loss (Pips):		Strategy:		Notes:		

Date:		Time Open:		Time Closed:		
Currency Pair	Buy / Sell	Trade Size	Entry Price	Target Price	Stop Loss	Closing Price
Profit /Loss (Pips):		Strategy:		Notes:		

Date:		Time Open:		Time Closed:		
Currency Pair	Buy / Sell	Trade Size	Entry Price	Target Price	Stop Loss	Closing Price
Profit /Loss (Pips):		Strategy:		Notes:		

Date:		Time Open:		Time Closed:		
Currency Pair	Buy / Sell	Trade Size	Entry Price	Target Price	Stop Loss	Closing Price
Profit /Loss (Pips):		Strategy:		Notes:		

Date:		Time Open:		Time Closed:		
Currency Pair	Buy / Sell	Trade Size	Entry Price	Target Price	Stop Loss	Closing Price
Profit /Loss (Pips):		Strategy:		Notes:		

Date:		Time Open:		Time Closed:		
Currency Pair	Buy / Sell	Trade Size	Entry Price	Target Price	Stop Loss	Closing Price
Profit /Loss (Pips):		Strategy:		Notes:		

Date:		Time Open:		Time Closed:		
Currency Pair	Buy / Sell	Trade Size	Entry Price	Target Price	Stop Loss	Closing Price
Profit /Loss (Pips):		Strategy:		Notes:		

Date:		Time Open:		Time Closed:		
Currency Pair	Buy / Sell	Trade Size	Entry Price	Target Price	Stop Loss	Closing Price
Profit /Loss (Pips):		Strategy:		Notes:		

Date:		Time Open:		Time Closed:		
Currency Pair	Buy / Sell	Trade Size	Entry Price	Target Price	Stop Loss	Closing Price
Profit /Loss (Pips):		Strategy:		Notes:		

Date:		Time Open:		Time Closed:		
Currency Pair	Buy / Sell	Trade Size	Entry Price	Target Price	Stop Loss	Closing Price
Profit /Loss (Pips):		Strategy:		Notes:		

Date:		Time Open:		Time Closed:		
Currency Pair	Buy / Sell	Trade Size	Entry Price	Target Price	Stop Loss	Closing Price
Profit /Loss (Pips):		Strategy:		Notes:		

Date:		Time Open:		Time Closed:		
Currency Pair	Buy / Sell	Trade Size	Entry Price	Target Price	Stop Loss	Closing Price
Profit /Loss (Pips):		Strategy:		Notes:		

Date:		Time Open:		Time Closed:		
Currency Pair	Buy / Sell	Trade Size	Entry Price	Target Price	Stop Loss	Closing Price
Profit /Loss (Pips):		Strategy:		Notes:		

Date:		Time Open:		Time Closed:		
Currency Pair	Buy / Sell	Trade Size	Entry Price	Target Price	Stop Loss	Closing Price
Profit /Loss (Pips):		Strategy:		Notes:		

Date:		Time Open:		Time Closed:		
Currency Pair	Buy / Sell	Trade Size	Entry Price	Target Price	Stop Loss	Closing Price
Profit /Loss (Pips):		Strategy:		Notes:		

Date:		Time Open:		Time Closed:		
Currency Pair	Buy / Sell	Trade Size	Entry Price	Target Price	Stop Loss	Closing Price
Profit /Loss (Pips):		Strategy:		Notes:		

Date:		Time Open:		Time Closed:		
Currency Pair	Buy / Sell	Trade Size	Entry Price	Target Price	Stop Loss	Closing Price
Profit /Loss (Pips):		Strategy:		Notes:		

Date:		Time Open:		Time Closed:		
Currency Pair	Buy / Sell	Trade Size	Entry Price	Target Price	Stop Loss	Closing Price
Profit /Loss (Pips):		Strategy:		Notes:		

Date:		Time Open:		Time Closed:		
Currency Pair	Buy / Sell	Trade Size	Entry Price	Target Price	Stop Loss	Closing Price
Profit /Loss (Pips):		Strategy:		Notes:		

Date:		Time Open:		Time Closed:		
Currency Pair	Buy / Sell	Trade Size	Entry Price	Target Price	Stop Loss	Closing Price
Profit /Loss (Pips):		Strategy:		Notes:		

Date:		Time Open:		Time Closed:		
Currency Pair	Buy / Sell	Trade Size	Entry Price	Target Price	Stop Loss	Closing Price
Profit /Loss (Pips):		Strategy:		Notes:		

Date:		Time Open:		Time Closed:		
Currency Pair	Buy / Sell	Trade Size	Entry Price	Target Price	Stop Loss	Closing Price
Profit /Loss (Pips):		Strategy:		Notes:		

Date:		Time Open:		Time Closed:		
Currency Pair	Buy / Sell	Trade Size	Entry Price	Target Price	Stop Loss	Closing Price
Profit /Loss (Pips):		Strategy:		Notes:		

Date:		Time Open:		Time Closed:		
Currency Pair	Buy / Sell	Trade Size	Entry Price	Target Price	Stop Loss	Closing Price
Profit /Loss (Pips):		Strategy:		Notes:		

Date:		Time Open:		Time Closed:		
Currency Pair	Buy / Sell	Trade Size	Entry Price	Target Price	Stop Loss	Closing Price
Profit /Loss (Pips):		Strategy:		Notes:		

Date:		Time Open:		Time Closed:		
Currency Pair	Buy / Sell	Trade Size	Entry Price	Target Price	Stop Loss	Closing Price
Profit /Loss (Pips):		Strategy:		Notes:		

Date:		Time Open:		Time Closed:		
Currency Pair	Buy / Sell	Trade Size	Entry Price	Target Price	Stop Loss	Closing Price
Profit /Loss (Pips):		Strategy:		Notes:		

Date:		Time Open:		Time Closed:		
Currency Pair	Buy / Sell	Trade Size	Entry Price	Target Price	Stop Loss	Closing Price
Profit /Loss (Pips):		Strategy:		Notes:		

Date:		Time Open:		Time Closed:		
Currency Pair	Buy / Sell	Trade Size	Entry Price	Target Price	Stop Loss	Closing Price
Profit /Loss (Pips):		Strategy:		Notes:		

Date:		Time Open:		Time Closed:		
Currency Pair	Buy / Sell	Trade Size	Entry Price	Target Price	Stop Loss	Closing Price
Profit /Loss (Pips):		Strategy:		Notes:		

Date:		Time Open:		Time Closed:		
Currency Pair	Buy / Sell	Trade Size	Entry Price	Target Price	Stop Loss	Closing Price
Profit /Loss (Pips):		Strategy:		Notes:		

Date:		Time Open:		Time Closed:		
Currency Pair	Buy / Sell	Trade Size	Entry Price	Target Price	Stop Loss	Closing Price
Profit /Loss (Pips):		Strategy:		Notes:		

Date:		Time Open:		Time Closed:		
Currency Pair	Buy / Sell	Trade Size	Entry Price	Target Price	Stop Loss	Closing Price
Profit /Loss (Pips):		Strategy:		Notes:		

Date:		Time Open:		Time Closed:		
Currency Pair	Buy / Sell	Trade Size	Entry Price	Target Price	Stop Loss	Closing Price
Profit /Loss (Pips):		Strategy:		Notes:		

Date:		Time Open:		Time Closed:		
Currency Pair	Buy / Sell	Trade Size	Entry Price	Target Price	Stop Loss	Closing Price
Profit /Loss (Pips):		Strategy:		Notes:		

Date:		Time Open:		Time Closed:		
Currency Pair	Buy / Sell	Trade Size	Entry Price	Target Price	Stop Loss	Closing Price
Profit /Loss (Pips):		Strategy:		Notes:		

Date:		Time Open:		Time Closed:		
Currency Pair	Buy / Sell	Trade Size	Entry Price	Target Price	Stop Loss	Closing Price
Profit /Loss (Pips):		Strategy:		Notes:		

Date:		Time Open:		Time Closed:		
Currency Pair	Buy / Sell	Trade Size	Entry Price	Target Price	Stop Loss	Closing Price
Profit /Loss (Pips):		Strategy:		Notes:		

Date:		Time Open:		Time Closed:		
Currency Pair	Buy / Sell	Trade Size	Entry Price	Target Price	Stop Loss	Closing Price
Profit /Loss (Pips):		Strategy:		Notes:		

Date:		Time Open:		Time Closed:		
Currency Pair	Buy / Sell	Trade Size	Entry Price	Target Price	Stop Loss	Closing Price
Profit /Loss (Pips):		Strategy:		Notes:		

Date:		Time Open:		Time Closed:		
Currency Pair	Buy / Sell	Trade Size	Entry Price	Target Price	Stop Loss	Closing Price
Profit /Loss (Pips):		Strategy:		Notes:		

Date:		Time Open:		Time Closed:		
Currency Pair	Buy / Sell	Trade Size	Entry Price	Target Price	Stop Loss	Closing Price
Profit /Loss (Pips):		Strategy:		Notes:		

Date:		Time Open:		Time Closed:		
Currency Pair	Buy / Sell	Trade Size	Entry Price	Target Price	Stop Loss	Closing Price
Profit /Loss (Pips):		Strategy:		Notes:		

Date:		Time Open:		Time Closed:		
Currency Pair	Buy / Sell	Trade Size	Entry Price	Target Price	Stop Loss	Closing Price
Profit /Loss (Pips):		Strategy:		Notes:		

Date:		Time Open:		Time Closed:		
Currency Pair	Buy / Sell	Trade Size	Entry Price	Target Price	Stop Loss	Closing Price
Profit /Loss (Pips):		Strategy:		Notes:		

Date:		Time Open:		Time Closed:		
Currency Pair	Buy / Sell	Trade Size	Entry Price	Target Price	Stop Loss	Closing Price
Profit /Loss (Pips):		Strategy:		Notes:		

Date:		Time Open:		Time Closed:		
Currency Pair	Buy / Sell	Trade Size	Entry Price	Target Price	Stop Loss	Closing Price
Profit /Loss (Pips):		Strategy:		Notes:		

Date:		Time Open:		Time Closed:		
Currency Pair	Buy / Sell	Trade Size	Entry Price	Target Price	Stop Loss	Closing Price
Profit /Loss (Pips):		Strategy:		Notes:		

Date:		Time Open:		Time Closed:		
Currency Pair	Buy / Sell	Trade Size	Entry Price	Target Price	Stop Loss	Closing Price
Profit /Loss (Pips):		Strategy:		Notes:		

Date:		Time Open:		Time Closed:		
Currency Pair	Buy / Sell	Trade Size	Entry Price	Target Price	Stop Loss	Closing Price
Profit /Loss (Pips):		Strategy:		Notes:		

Date:		Time Open:		Time Closed:		
Currency Pair	Buy / Sell	Trade Size	Entry Price	Target Price	Stop Loss	Closing Price
Profit /Loss (Pips):		Strategy:		Notes:		

Date:		Time Open:		Time Closed:		
Currency Pair	Buy / Sell	Trade Size	Entry Price	Target Price	Stop Loss	Closing Price
Profit /Loss (Pips):		Strategy:		Notes:		

Date:		Time Open:		Time Closed:		
Currency Pair	Buy / Sell	Trade Size	Entry Price	Target Price	Stop Loss	Closing Price
Profit /Loss (Pips):		Strategy:		Notes:		

Date:		Time Open:		Time Closed:		
Currency Pair	Buy / Sell	Trade Size	Entry Price	Target Price	Stop Loss	Closing Price
Profit /Loss (Pips):		Strategy:		Notes:		

Date:		Time Open:		Time Closed:		
Currency Pair	Buy / Sell	Trade Size	Entry Price	Target Price	Stop Loss	Closing Price
Profit /Loss (Pips):		Strategy:		Notes:		

Date:		Time Open:		Time Closed:		
Currency Pair	Buy / Sell	Trade Size	Entry Price	Target Price	Stop Loss	Closing Price
Profit /Loss (Pips):		Strategy:		Notes:		

Date:		Time Open:		Time Closed:		
Currency Pair	Buy / Sell	Trade Size	Entry Price	Target Price	Stop Loss	Closing Price
Profit /Loss (Pips):		Strategy:		Notes:		

Date:		Time Open:		Time Closed:		
Currency Pair	Buy / Sell	Trade Size	Entry Price	Target Price	Stop Loss	Closing Price
Profit /Loss (Pips):		Strategy:		Notes:		

Date:		Time Open:		Time Closed:		
Currency Pair	Buy / Sell	Trade Size	Entry Price	Target Price	Stop Loss	Closing Price
Profit /Loss (Pips):		Strategy:		Notes:		

Date:		Time Open:		Time Closed:		
Currency Pair	Buy / Sell	Trade Size	Entry Price	Target Price	Stop Loss	Closing Price
Profit /Loss (Pips):		Strategy:		Notes:		

Date:		Time Open:		Time Closed:		
Currency Pair	Buy / Sell	Trade Size	Entry Price	Target Price	Stop Loss	Closing Price
Profit /Loss (Pips):		Strategy:		Notes:		

Date:		Time Open:		Time Closed:		
Currency Pair	Buy / Sell	Trade Size	Entry Price	Target Price	Stop Loss	Closing Price
Profit /Loss (Pips):		Strategy:		Notes:		

Date:		Time Open:		Time Closed:		
Currency Pair	Buy / Sell	Trade Size	Entry Price	Target Price	Stop Loss	Closing Price
Profit /Loss (Pips):		Strategy:		Notes:		

Date:		Time Open:		Time Closed:		
Currency Pair	Buy / Sell	Trade Size	Entry Price	Target Price	Stop Loss	Closing Price
Profit /Loss (Pips):		Strategy:		Notes:		

Date:		Time Open:		Time Closed:		
Currency Pair	Buy / Sell	Trade Size	Entry Price	Target Price	Stop Loss	Closing Price
Profit /Loss (Pips):		Strategy:		Notes:		

Date:		Time Open:		Time Closed:		
Currency Pair	Buy / Sell	Trade Size	Entry Price	Target Price	Stop Loss	Closing Price
Profit /Loss (Pips):		Strategy:		Notes:		

Date:		Time Open:		Time Closed:		
Currency Pair	Buy / Sell	Trade Size	Entry Price	Target Price	Stop Loss	Closing Price
Profit /Loss (Pips):		Strategy:		Notes:		

Date:		Time Open:		Time Closed:		
Currency Pair	Buy / Sell	Trade Size	Entry Price	Target Price	Stop Loss	Closing Price
Profit /Loss (Pips):		Strategy:		Notes:		

Date:		Time Open:		Time Closed:		
Currency Pair	Buy / Sell	Trade Size	Entry Price	Target Price	Stop Loss	Closing Price
Profit /Loss (Pips):		Strategy:		Notes:		

Date:		Time Open:		Time Closed:		
Currency Pair	Buy / Sell	Trade Size	Entry Price	Target Price	Stop Loss	Closing Price
Profit /Loss (Pips):		Strategy:		Notes:		

Date:		Time Open:		Time Closed:		
Currency Pair	Buy / Sell	Trade Size	Entry Price	Target Price	Stop Loss	Closing Price
Profit /Loss (Pips):		Strategy:		Notes:		

Date:		Time Open:		Time Closed:		
Currency Pair	Buy / Sell	Trade Size	Entry Price	Target Price	Stop Loss	Closing Price
Profit /Loss (Pips):		Strategy:		Notes:		

Date:		Time Open:		Time Closed:		
Currency Pair	Buy / Sell	Trade Size	Entry Price	Target Price	Stop Loss	Closing Price
Profit /Loss (Pips):		Strategy:		Notes:		

Date:		Time Open:		Time Closed:		
Currency Pair	Buy / Sell	Trade Size	Entry Price	Target Price	Stop Loss	Closing Price
Profit /Loss (Pips):		Strategy:		Notes:		

Date:		Time Open:		Time Closed:		
Currency Pair	Buy / Sell	Trade Size	Entry Price	Target Price	Stop Loss	Closing Price
Profit /Loss (Pips):		Strategy:		Notes:		

Date:		Time Open:		Time Closed:		
Currency Pair	Buy / Sell	Trade Size	Entry Price	Target Price	Stop Loss	Closing Price
Profit /Loss (Pips):		Strategy:		Notes:		

Date:		Time Open:		Time Closed:		
Currency Pair	Buy / Sell	Trade Size	Entry Price	Target Price	Stop Loss	Closing Price
Profit /Loss (Pips):		Strategy:		Notes:		

Date:		Time Open:		Time Closed:		
Currency Pair	Buy / Sell	Trade Size	Entry Price	Target Price	Stop Loss	Closing Price
Profit /Loss (Pips):		Strategy:		Notes:		

Date:		Time Open:		Time Closed:		
Currency Pair	Buy / Sell	Trade Size	Entry Price	Target Price	Stop Loss	Closing Price
Profit /Loss (Pips):		Strategy:		Notes:		

Date:		Time Open:		Time Closed:		
Currency Pair	**Buy / Sell**	**Trade Size**	**Entry Price**	**Target Price**	**Stop Loss**	**Closing Price**
Profit /Loss (Pips):		Strategy:		Notes:		

Date:		Time Open:		Time Closed:		
Currency Pair	**Buy / Sell**	**Trade Size**	**Entry Price**	**Target Price**	**Stop Loss**	**Closing Price**
Profit /Loss (Pips):		Strategy:		Notes:		

Date:		Time Open:		Time Closed:		
Currency Pair	**Buy / Sell**	**Trade Size**	**Entry Price**	**Target Price**	**Stop Loss**	**Closing Price**
Profit /Loss (Pips):		Strategy:		Notes:		

Date:		Time Open:		Time Closed:		
Currency Pair	**Buy / Sell**	**Trade Size**	**Entry Price**	**Target Price**	**Stop Loss**	**Closing Price**
Profit /Loss (Pips):		Strategy:		Notes:		

Date:		Time Open:		Time Closed:		
Currency Pair	**Buy / Sell**	**Trade Size**	**Entry Price**	**Target Price**	**Stop Loss**	**Closing Price**
Profit /Loss (Pips):		Strategy:		Notes:		

Date:		Time Open:		Time Closed:		
Currency Pair	Buy / Sell	Trade Size	Entry Price	Target Price	Stop Loss	Closing Price
Profit /Loss (Pips):		Strategy:		Notes:		

Date:		Time Open:		Time Closed:		
Currency Pair	Buy / Sell	Trade Size	Entry Price	Target Price	Stop Loss	Closing Price
Profit /Loss (Pips):		Strategy:		Notes:		

Date:		Time Open:		Time Closed:		
Currency Pair	Buy / Sell	Trade Size	Entry Price	Target Price	Stop Loss	Closing Price
Profit /Loss (Pips):		Strategy:		Notes:		

Date:		Time Open:		Time Closed:		
Currency Pair	Buy / Sell	Trade Size	Entry Price	Target Price	Stop Loss	Closing Price
Profit /Loss (Pips):		Strategy:		Notes:		

Date:		Time Open:		Time Closed:		
Currency Pair	Buy / Sell	Trade Size	Entry Price	Target Price	Stop Loss	Closing Price
Profit /Loss (Pips):		Strategy:		Notes:		

Date:		Time Open:		Time Closed:		
Currency Pair	Buy / Sell	Trade Size	Entry Price	Target Price	Stop Loss	Closing Price
Profit /Loss (Pips):		Strategy:		Notes:		

Date:		Time Open:		Time Closed:		
Currency Pair	Buy / Sell	Trade Size	Entry Price	Target Price	Stop Loss	Closing Price
Profit /Loss (Pips):		Strategy:		Notes:		

Date:		Time Open:		Time Closed:		
Currency Pair	Buy / Sell	Trade Size	Entry Price	Target Price	Stop Loss	Closing Price
Profit /Loss (Pips):		Strategy:		Notes:		

Date:		Time Open:		Time Closed:		
Currency Pair	Buy / Sell	Trade Size	Entry Price	Target Price	Stop Loss	Closing Price
Profit /Loss (Pips):		Strategy:		Notes:		

Date:		Time Open:		Time Closed:		
Currency Pair	Buy / Sell	Trade Size	Entry Price	Target Price	Stop Loss	Closing Price
Profit /Loss (Pips):		Strategy:		Notes:		

Date:		Time Open:		Time Closed:		
Currency Pair	Buy / Sell	Trade Size	Entry Price	Target Price	Stop Loss	Closing Price
Profit /Loss (Pips):		Strategy:		Notes:		

Date:		Time Open:		Time Closed:		
Currency Pair	Buy / Sell	Trade Size	Entry Price	Target Price	Stop Loss	Closing Price
Profit /Loss (Pips):		Strategy:		Notes:		

Date:		Time Open:		Time Closed:		
Currency Pair	Buy / Sell	Trade Size	Entry Price	Target Price	Stop Loss	Closing Price
Profit /Loss (Pips):		Strategy:		Notes:		

Date:		Time Open:		Time Closed:		
Currency Pair	Buy / Sell	Trade Size	Entry Price	Target Price	Stop Loss	Closing Price
Profit /Loss (Pips):		Strategy:		Notes:		

Date:		Time Open:		Time Closed:		
Currency Pair	Buy / Sell	Trade Size	Entry Price	Target Price	Stop Loss	Closing Price
Profit /Loss (Pips):		Strategy:		Notes:		

Date:		Time Open:		Time Closed:		
Currency Pair	Buy / Sell	Trade Size	Entry Price	Target Price	Stop Loss	Closing Price
Profit /Loss (Pips):		Strategy:		Notes:		

Date:		Time Open:		Time Closed:		
Currency Pair	Buy / Sell	Trade Size	Entry Price	Target Price	Stop Loss	Closing Price
Profit /Loss (Pips):		Strategy:		Notes:		

Date:		Time Open:		Time Closed:		
Currency Pair	Buy / Sell	Trade Size	Entry Price	Target Price	Stop Loss	Closing Price
Profit /Loss (Pips):		Strategy:		Notes:		

Date:		Time Open:		Time Closed:		
Currency Pair	Buy / Sell	Trade Size	Entry Price	Target Price	Stop Loss	Closing Price
Profit /Loss (Pips):		Strategy:		Notes:		

Date:		Time Open:		Time Closed:		
Currency Pair	Buy / Sell	Trade Size	Entry Price	Target Price	Stop Loss	Closing Price
Profit /Loss (Pips):		Strategy:		Notes:		

Date:		Time Open:		Time Closed:		
Currency Pair	Buy / Sell	Trade Size	Entry Price	Target Price	Stop Loss	Closing Price
Profit /Loss (Pips):		Strategy:		Notes:		

Date:		Time Open:		Time Closed:		
Currency Pair	Buy / Sell	Trade Size	Entry Price	Target Price	Stop Loss	Closing Price
Profit /Loss (Pips):		Strategy:		Notes:		

Date:		Time Open:		Time Closed:		
Currency Pair	Buy / Sell	Trade Size	Entry Price	Target Price	Stop Loss	Closing Price
Profit /Loss (Pips):		Strategy:		Notes:		

Date:		Time Open:		Time Closed:		
Currency Pair	Buy / Sell	Trade Size	Entry Price	Target Price	Stop Loss	Closing Price
Profit /Loss (Pips):		Strategy:		Notes:		

Date:		Time Open:		Time Closed:		
Currency Pair	Buy / Sell	Trade Size	Entry Price	Target Price	Stop Loss	Closing Price
Profit /Loss (Pips):		Strategy:		Notes:		

Date:		Time Open:		Time Closed:		
Currency Pair	**Buy / Sell**	**Trade Size**	**Entry Price**	**Target Price**	**Stop Loss**	**Closing Price**
Profit /Loss (Pips):		Strategy:		Notes:		

Date:		Time Open:		Time Closed:		
Currency Pair	**Buy / Sell**	**Trade Size**	**Entry Price**	**Target Price**	**Stop Loss**	**Closing Price**
Profit /Loss (Pips):		Strategy:		Notes:		

Date:		Time Open:		Time Closed:		
Currency Pair	**Buy / Sell**	**Trade Size**	**Entry Price**	**Target Price**	**Stop Loss**	**Closing Price**
Profit /Loss (Pips):		Strategy:		Notes:		

Date:		Time Open:		Time Closed:		
Currency Pair	**Buy / Sell**	**Trade Size**	**Entry Price**	**Target Price**	**Stop Loss**	**Closing Price**
Profit /Loss (Pips):		Strategy:		Notes:		

Date:		Time Open:		Time Closed:		
Currency Pair	**Buy / Sell**	**Trade Size**	**Entry Price**	**Target Price**	**Stop Loss**	**Closing Price**
Profit /Loss (Pips):		Strategy:		Notes:		

Date:		Time Open:		Time Closed:		
Currency Pair	**Buy / Sell**	**Trade Size**	**Entry Price**	**Target Price**	**Stop Loss**	**Closing Price**
Profit /Loss (Pips):		Strategy:		Notes:		

Date:		Time Open:		Time Closed:		
Currency Pair	**Buy / Sell**	**Trade Size**	**Entry Price**	**Target Price**	**Stop Loss**	**Closing Price**
Profit /Loss (Pips):		Strategy:		Notes:		

Date:		Time Open:		Time Closed:		
Currency Pair	**Buy / Sell**	**Trade Size**	**Entry Price**	**Target Price**	**Stop Loss**	**Closing Price**
Profit /Loss (Pips):		Strategy:		Notes:		

Date:		Time Open:		Time Closed:		
Currency Pair	**Buy / Sell**	**Trade Size**	**Entry Price**	**Target Price**	**Stop Loss**	**Closing Price**
Profit /Loss (Pips):		Strategy:		Notes:		

Date:		Time Open:		Time Closed:		
Currency Pair	**Buy / Sell**	**Trade Size**	**Entry Price**	**Target Price**	**Stop Loss**	**Closing Price**
Profit /Loss (Pips):		Strategy:		Notes:		

Date:		Time Open:		Time Closed:		
Currency Pair	Buy / Sell	Trade Size	Entry Price	Target Price	Stop Loss	Closing Price
Profit /Loss (Pips):		Strategy:		Notes:		

Date:		Time Open:		Time Closed:		
Currency Pair	Buy / Sell	Trade Size	Entry Price	Target Price	Stop Loss	Closing Price
Profit /Loss (Pips):		Strategy:		Notes:		

Date:		Time Open:		Time Closed:		
Currency Pair	Buy / Sell	Trade Size	Entry Price	Target Price	Stop Loss	Closing Price
Profit /Loss (Pips):		Strategy:		Notes:		

Date:		Time Open:		Time Closed:		
Currency Pair	Buy / Sell	Trade Size	Entry Price	Target Price	Stop Loss	Closing Price
Profit /Loss (Pips):		Strategy:		Notes:		

Date:		Time Open:		Time Closed:		
Currency Pair	Buy / Sell	Trade Size	Entry Price	Target Price	Stop Loss	Closing Price
Profit /Loss (Pips):		Strategy:		Notes:		

Date:		Time Open:		Time Closed:		
Currency Pair	Buy / Sell	Trade Size	Entry Price	Target Price	Stop Loss	Closing Price
Profit /Loss (Pips):		Strategy:		Notes:		

Date:		Time Open:		Time Closed:		
Currency Pair	Buy / Sell	Trade Size	Entry Price	Target Price	Stop Loss	Closing Price
Profit /Loss (Pips):		Strategy:		Notes:		

Date:		Time Open:		Time Closed:		
Currency Pair	Buy / Sell	Trade Size	Entry Price	Target Price	Stop Loss	Closing Price
Profit /Loss (Pips):		Strategy:		Notes:		

Date:		Time Open:		Time Closed:		
Currency Pair	Buy / Sell	Trade Size	Entry Price	Target Price	Stop Loss	Closing Price
Profit /Loss (Pips):		Strategy:		Notes:		

Date:		Time Open:		Time Closed:		
Currency Pair	Buy / Sell	Trade Size	Entry Price	Target Price	Stop Loss	Closing Price
Profit /Loss (Pips):		Strategy:		Notes:		

Date:		Time Open:		Time Closed:		
Currency Pair	Buy / Sell	Trade Size	Entry Price	Target Price	Stop Loss	Closing Price
Profit /Loss (Pips):		Strategy:		Notes:		

Date:		Time Open:		Time Closed:		
Currency Pair	Buy / Sell	Trade Size	Entry Price	Target Price	Stop Loss	Closing Price
Profit /Loss (Pips):		Strategy:		Notes:		

Date:		Time Open:		Time Closed:		
Currency Pair	Buy / Sell	Trade Size	Entry Price	Target Price	Stop Loss	Closing Price
Profit /Loss (Pips):		Strategy:		Notes:		

Date:		Time Open:		Time Closed:		
Currency Pair	Buy / Sell	Trade Size	Entry Price	Target Price	Stop Loss	Closing Price
Profit /Loss (Pips):		Strategy:		Notes:		

Date:		Time Open:		Time Closed:		
Currency Pair	Buy / Sell	Trade Size	Entry Price	Target Price	Stop Loss	Closing Price
Profit /Loss (Pips):		Strategy:		Notes:		

Date:		Time Open:		Time Closed:		
Currency Pair	**Buy / Sell**	**Trade Size**	**Entry Price**	**Target Price**	**Stop Loss**	**Closing Price**
Profit /Loss (Pips):		Strategy:		Notes:		

Date:		Time Open:		Time Closed:		
Currency Pair	**Buy / Sell**	**Trade Size**	**Entry Price**	**Target Price**	**Stop Loss**	**Closing Price**
Profit /Loss (Pips):		Strategy:		Notes:		

Date:		Time Open:		Time Closed:		
Currency Pair	**Buy / Sell**	**Trade Size**	**Entry Price**	**Target Price**	**Stop Loss**	**Closing Price**
Profit /Loss (Pips):		Strategy:		Notes:		

Date:		Time Open:		Time Closed:		
Currency Pair	**Buy / Sell**	**Trade Size**	**Entry Price**	**Target Price**	**Stop Loss**	**Closing Price**
Profit /Loss (Pips):		Strategy:		Notes:		

Date:		Time Open:		Time Closed:		
Currency Pair	**Buy / Sell**	**Trade Size**	**Entry Price**	**Target Price**	**Stop Loss**	**Closing Price**
Profit /Loss (Pips):		Strategy:		Notes:		

Date:		Time Open:		Time Closed:		
Currency Pair	**Buy / Sell**	**Trade Size**	**Entry Price**	**Target Price**	**Stop Loss**	**Closing Price**
Profit /Loss (Pips):		Strategy:		Notes:		

Date:		Time Open:		Time Closed:		
Currency Pair	**Buy / Sell**	**Trade Size**	**Entry Price**	**Target Price**	**Stop Loss**	**Closing Price**
Profit /Loss (Pips):		Strategy:		Notes:		

Date:		Time Open:		Time Closed:		
Currency Pair	**Buy / Sell**	**Trade Size**	**Entry Price**	**Target Price**	**Stop Loss**	**Closing Price**
Profit /Loss (Pips):		Strategy:		Notes:		

Date:		Time Open:		Time Closed:		
Currency Pair	**Buy / Sell**	**Trade Size**	**Entry Price**	**Target Price**	**Stop Loss**	**Closing Price**
Profit /Loss (Pips):		Strategy:		Notes:		

Date:		Time Open:		Time Closed:		
Currency Pair	**Buy / Sell**	**Trade Size**	**Entry Price**	**Target Price**	**Stop Loss**	**Closing Price**
Profit /Loss (Pips):		Strategy:		Notes:		

Date:		Time Open:		Time Closed:		
Currency Pair	Buy / Sell	Trade Size	Entry Price	Target Price	Stop Loss	Closing Price

Profit /Loss (Pips):	Strategy:	Notes:

Date:		Time Open:		Time Closed:		
Currency Pair	Buy / Sell	Trade Size	Entry Price	Target Price	Stop Loss	Closing Price

Profit /Loss (Pips):	Strategy:	Notes:

Date:		Time Open:		Time Closed:		
Currency Pair	Buy / Sell	Trade Size	Entry Price	Target Price	Stop Loss	Closing Price

Profit /Loss (Pips):	Strategy:	Notes:

Date:		Time Open:		Time Closed:		
Currency Pair	Buy / Sell	Trade Size	Entry Price	Target Price	Stop Loss	Closing Price

Profit /Loss (Pips):	Strategy:	Notes:

Date:		Time Open:		Time Closed:		
Currency Pair	Buy / Sell	Trade Size	Entry Price	Target Price	Stop Loss	Closing Price

Profit /Loss (Pips):	Strategy:	Notes:

Date:		Time Open:		Time Closed:		
Currency Pair	Buy / Sell	Trade Size	Entry Price	Target Price	Stop Loss	Closing Price
Profit /Loss (Pips):		Strategy:		Notes:		

Date:		Time Open:		Time Closed:		
Currency Pair	Buy / Sell	Trade Size	Entry Price	Target Price	Stop Loss	Closing Price
Profit /Loss (Pips):		Strategy:		Notes:		

Date:		Time Open:		Time Closed:		
Currency Pair	Buy / Sell	Trade Size	Entry Price	Target Price	Stop Loss	Closing Price
Profit /Loss (Pips):		Strategy:		Notes:		

Date:		Time Open:		Time Closed:		
Currency Pair	Buy / Sell	Trade Size	Entry Price	Target Price	Stop Loss	Closing Price
Profit /Loss (Pips):		Strategy:		Notes:		

Date:		Time Open:		Time Closed:		
Currency Pair	Buy / Sell	Trade Size	Entry Price	Target Price	Stop Loss	Closing Price
Profit /Loss (Pips):		Strategy:		Notes:		

Date:		Time Open:		Time Closed:		
Currency Pair	**Buy / Sell**	**Trade Size**	**Entry Price**	**Target Price**	**Stop Loss**	**Closing Price**
Profit /Loss (Pips):		Strategy:		Notes:		

Date:		Time Open:		Time Closed:		
Currency Pair	**Buy / Sell**	**Trade Size**	**Entry Price**	**Target Price**	**Stop Loss**	**Closing Price**
Profit /Loss (Pips):		Strategy:		Notes:		

Date:		Time Open:		Time Closed:		
Currency Pair	**Buy / Sell**	**Trade Size**	**Entry Price**	**Target Price**	**Stop Loss**	**Closing Price**
Profit /Loss (Pips):		Strategy:		Notes:		

Date:		Time Open:		Time Closed:		
Currency Pair	**Buy / Sell**	**Trade Size**	**Entry Price**	**Target Price**	**Stop Loss**	**Closing Price**
Profit /Loss (Pips):		Strategy:		Notes:		

Date:		Time Open:		Time Closed:		
Currency Pair	**Buy / Sell**	**Trade Size**	**Entry Price**	**Target Price**	**Stop Loss**	**Closing Price**
Profit /Loss (Pips):		Strategy:		Notes:		

Date:		Time Open:		Time Closed:		
Currency Pair	Buy / Sell	Trade Size	Entry Price	Target Price	Stop Loss	Closing Price
Profit /Loss (Pips):		Strategy:		Notes:		

Date:		Time Open:		Time Closed:		
Currency Pair	Buy / Sell	Trade Size	Entry Price	Target Price	Stop Loss	Closing Price
Profit /Loss (Pips):		Strategy:		Notes:		

Date:		Time Open:		Time Closed:		
Currency Pair	Buy / Sell	Trade Size	Entry Price	Target Price	Stop Loss	Closing Price
Profit /Loss (Pips):		Strategy:		Notes:		

Date:		Time Open:		Time Closed:		
Currency Pair	Buy / Sell	Trade Size	Entry Price	Target Price	Stop Loss	Closing Price
Profit /Loss (Pips):		Strategy:		Notes:		

Date:		Time Open:		Time Closed:		
Currency Pair	Buy / Sell	Trade Size	Entry Price	Target Price	Stop Loss	Closing Price
Profit /Loss (Pips):		Strategy:		Notes:		

Date:		Time Open:		Time Closed:		
Currency Pair	**Buy / Sell**	**Trade Size**	**Entry Price**	**Target Price**	**Stop Loss**	**Closing Price**
Profit /Loss (Pips):		Strategy:		Notes:		

Date:		Time Open:		Time Closed:		
Currency Pair	**Buy / Sell**	**Trade Size**	**Entry Price**	**Target Price**	**Stop Loss**	**Closing Price**
Profit /Loss (Pips):		Strategy:		Notes:		

Date:		Time Open:		Time Closed:		
Currency Pair	**Buy / Sell**	**Trade Size**	**Entry Price**	**Target Price**	**Stop Loss**	**Closing Price**
Profit /Loss (Pips):		Strategy:		Notes:		

Date:		Time Open:		Time Closed:		
Currency Pair	**Buy / Sell**	**Trade Size**	**Entry Price**	**Target Price**	**Stop Loss**	**Closing Price**
Profit /Loss (Pips):		Strategy:		Notes:		

Date:		Time Open:		Time Closed:		
Currency Pair	**Buy / Sell**	**Trade Size**	**Entry Price**	**Target Price**	**Stop Loss**	**Closing Price**
Profit /Loss (Pips):		Strategy:		Notes:		

Date:		Time Open:		Time Closed:		
Currency Pair	Buy / Sell	Trade Size	Entry Price	Target Price	Stop Loss	Closing Price
Profit /Loss (Pips):		Strategy:		Notes:		

Date:		Time Open:		Time Closed:		
Currency Pair	Buy / Sell	Trade Size	Entry Price	Target Price	Stop Loss	Closing Price
Profit /Loss (Pips):		Strategy:		Notes:		

Date:		Time Open:		Time Closed:		
Currency Pair	Buy / Sell	Trade Size	Entry Price	Target Price	Stop Loss	Closing Price
Profit /Loss (Pips):		Strategy:		Notes:		

Date:		Time Open:		Time Closed:		
Currency Pair	Buy / Sell	Trade Size	Entry Price	Target Price	Stop Loss	Closing Price
Profit /Loss (Pips):		Strategy:		Notes:		

Date:		Time Open:		Time Closed:		
Currency Pair	Buy / Sell	Trade Size	Entry Price	Target Price	Stop Loss	Closing Price
Profit /Loss (Pips):		Strategy:		Notes:		

Date:		Time Open:		Time Closed:		
Currency Pair	Buy / Sell	Trade Size	Entry Price	Target Price	Stop Loss	Closing Price
Profit /Loss (Pips):		Strategy:		Notes:		

Date:		Time Open:		Time Closed:		
Currency Pair	Buy / Sell	Trade Size	Entry Price	Target Price	Stop Loss	Closing Price
Profit /Loss (Pips):		Strategy:		Notes:		

Date:		Time Open:		Time Closed:		
Currency Pair	Buy / Sell	Trade Size	Entry Price	Target Price	Stop Loss	Closing Price
Profit /Loss (Pips):		Strategy:		Notes:		

Date:		Time Open:		Time Closed:		
Currency Pair	Buy / Sell	Trade Size	Entry Price	Target Price	Stop Loss	Closing Price
Profit /Loss (Pips):		Strategy:		Notes:		

Date:		Time Open:		Time Closed:		
Currency Pair	Buy / Sell	Trade Size	Entry Price	Target Price	Stop Loss	Closing Price
Profit /Loss (Pips):		Strategy:		Notes:		

Date:		Time Open:		Time Closed:		
Currency Pair	Buy / Sell	Trade Size	Entry Price	Target Price	Stop Loss	Closing Price
Profit /Loss (Pips):		Strategy:		Notes:		

Date:		Time Open:		Time Closed:		
Currency Pair	Buy / Sell	Trade Size	Entry Price	Target Price	Stop Loss	Closing Price
Profit /Loss (Pips):		Strategy:		Notes:		

Date:		Time Open:		Time Closed:		
Currency Pair	Buy / Sell	Trade Size	Entry Price	Target Price	Stop Loss	Closing Price
Profit /Loss (Pips):		Strategy:		Notes:		

Date:		Time Open:		Time Closed:		
Currency Pair	Buy / Sell	Trade Size	Entry Price	Target Price	Stop Loss	Closing Price
Profit /Loss (Pips):		Strategy:		Notes:		

Date:		Time Open:		Time Closed:		
Currency Pair	Buy / Sell	Trade Size	Entry Price	Target Price	Stop Loss	Closing Price
Profit /Loss (Pips):		Strategy:		Notes:		

Date:		Time Open:		Time Closed:		
Currency Pair	Buy / Sell	Trade Size	Entry Price	Target Price	Stop Loss	Closing Price
Profit /Loss (Pips):		Strategy:		Notes:		

Date:		Time Open:		Time Closed:		
Currency Pair	Buy / Sell	Trade Size	Entry Price	Target Price	Stop Loss	Closing Price
Profit /Loss (Pips):		Strategy:		Notes:		

Date:		Time Open:		Time Closed:		
Currency Pair	Buy / Sell	Trade Size	Entry Price	Target Price	Stop Loss	Closing Price
Profit /Loss (Pips):		Strategy:		Notes:		

Date:		Time Open:		Time Closed:		
Currency Pair	Buy / Sell	Trade Size	Entry Price	Target Price	Stop Loss	Closing Price
Profit /Loss (Pips):		Strategy:		Notes:		

Date:		Time Open:		Time Closed:		
Currency Pair	Buy / Sell	Trade Size	Entry Price	Target Price	Stop Loss	Closing Price
Profit /Loss (Pips):		Strategy:		Notes:		

Date:		Time Open:		Time Closed:		
Currency Pair	Buy / Sell	Trade Size	Entry Price	Target Price	Stop Loss	Closing Price
Profit /Loss (Pips):		Strategy:		Notes:		

Date:		Time Open:		Time Closed:		
Currency Pair	Buy / Sell	Trade Size	Entry Price	Target Price	Stop Loss	Closing Price
Profit /Loss (Pips):		Strategy:		Notes:		

Date:		Time Open:		Time Closed:		
Currency Pair	Buy / Sell	Trade Size	Entry Price	Target Price	Stop Loss	Closing Price
Profit /Loss (Pips):		Strategy:		Notes:		

Date:		Time Open:		Time Closed:		
Currency Pair	Buy / Sell	Trade Size	Entry Price	Target Price	Stop Loss	Closing Price
Profit /Loss (Pips):		Strategy:		Notes:		

Date:		Time Open:		Time Closed:		
Currency Pair	Buy / Sell	Trade Size	Entry Price	Target Price	Stop Loss	Closing Price
Profit /Loss (Pips):		Strategy:		Notes:		

Date:		Time Open:		Time Closed:		
Currency Pair	Buy / Sell	Trade Size	Entry Price	Target Price	Stop Loss	Closing Price
Profit /Loss (Pips):		Strategy:		Notes:		

Date:		Time Open:		Time Closed:		
Currency Pair	Buy / Sell	Trade Size	Entry Price	Target Price	Stop Loss	Closing Price
Profit /Loss (Pips):		Strategy:		Notes:		

Date:		Time Open:		Time Closed:		
Currency Pair	Buy / Sell	Trade Size	Entry Price	Target Price	Stop Loss	Closing Price
Profit /Loss (Pips):		Strategy:		Notes:		

Date:		Time Open:		Time Closed:		
Currency Pair	Buy / Sell	Trade Size	Entry Price	Target Price	Stop Loss	Closing Price
Profit /Loss (Pips):		Strategy:		Notes:		

Date:		Time Open:		Time Closed:		
Currency Pair	Buy / Sell	Trade Size	Entry Price	Target Price	Stop Loss	Closing Price
Profit /Loss (Pips):		Strategy:		Notes:		

Date:		Time Open:		Time Closed:		
Currency Pair	Buy / Sell	Trade Size	Entry Price	Target Price	Stop Loss	Closing Price
Profit /Loss (Pips):		Strategy:		Notes:		

Date:		Time Open:		Time Closed:		
Currency Pair	Buy / Sell	Trade Size	Entry Price	Target Price	Stop Loss	Closing Price
Profit /Loss (Pips):		Strategy:		Notes:		

Date:		Time Open:		Time Closed:		
Currency Pair	Buy / Sell	Trade Size	Entry Price	Target Price	Stop Loss	Closing Price
Profit /Loss (Pips):		Strategy:		Notes:		

Date:		Time Open:		Time Closed:		
Currency Pair	Buy / Sell	Trade Size	Entry Price	Target Price	Stop Loss	Closing Price
Profit /Loss (Pips):		Strategy:		Notes:		

Date:		Time Open:		Time Closed:		
Currency Pair	Buy / Sell	Trade Size	Entry Price	Target Price	Stop Loss	Closing Price
Profit /Loss (Pips):		Strategy:		Notes:		

Date:		Time Open:		Time Closed:		
Currency Pair	Buy / Sell	Trade Size	Entry Price	Target Price	Stop Loss	Closing Price
Profit /Loss (Pips):		Strategy:		Notes:		

Date:		Time Open:		Time Closed:		
Currency Pair	Buy / Sell	Trade Size	Entry Price	Target Price	Stop Loss	Closing Price
Profit /Loss (Pips):		Strategy:		Notes:		

Date:		Time Open:		Time Closed:		
Currency Pair	Buy / Sell	Trade Size	Entry Price	Target Price	Stop Loss	Closing Price
Profit /Loss (Pips):		Strategy:		Notes:		

Date:		Time Open:		Time Closed:		
Currency Pair	Buy / Sell	Trade Size	Entry Price	Target Price	Stop Loss	Closing Price
Profit /Loss (Pips):		Strategy:		Notes:		

Date:		Time Open:		Time Closed:		
Currency Pair	Buy / Sell	Trade Size	Entry Price	Target Price	Stop Loss	Closing Price
Profit /Loss (Pips):		Strategy:		Notes:		

Date:		Time Open:		Time Closed:		
Currency Pair	Buy / Sell	Trade Size	Entry Price	Target Price	Stop Loss	Closing Price
Profit /Loss (Pips):		Strategy:		Notes:		

Date:		Time Open:		Time Closed:		
Currency Pair	Buy / Sell	Trade Size	Entry Price	Target Price	Stop Loss	Closing Price
Profit /Loss (Pips):		Strategy:		Notes:		

Date:		Time Open:		Time Closed:		
Currency Pair	Buy / Sell	Trade Size	Entry Price	Target Price	Stop Loss	Closing Price
Profit /Loss (Pips):		Strategy:		Notes:		

Date:		Time Open:		Time Closed:		
Currency Pair	Buy / Sell	Trade Size	Entry Price	Target Price	Stop Loss	Closing Price
Profit /Loss (Pips):		Strategy:		Notes:		

Date:		Time Open:		Time Closed:		
Currency Pair	Buy / Sell	Trade Size	Entry Price	Target Price	Stop Loss	Closing Price
Profit /Loss (Pips):		Strategy:		Notes:		

Date:		Time Open:		Time Closed:		
Currency Pair	Buy / Sell	Trade Size	Entry Price	Target Price	Stop Loss	Closing Price
Profit /Loss (Pips):		Strategy:		Notes:		

Date:		Time Open:		Time Closed:		
Currency Pair	Buy / Sell	Trade Size	Entry Price	Target Price	Stop Loss	Closing Price
Profit /Loss (Pips):		Strategy:		Notes:		

Date:		Time Open:		Time Closed:		
Currency Pair	Buy / Sell	Trade Size	Entry Price	Target Price	Stop Loss	Closing Price
Profit /Loss (Pips):		Strategy:		Notes:		

Date:		Time Open:		Time Closed:		
Currency Pair	Buy / Sell	Trade Size	Entry Price	Target Price	Stop Loss	Closing Price
Profit /Loss (Pips):		Strategy:		Notes:		

Date:		Time Open:		Time Closed:		
Currency Pair	Buy / Sell	Trade Size	Entry Price	Target Price	Stop Loss	Closing Price
Profit /Loss (Pips):		Strategy:		Notes:		

Date:		Time Open:		Time Closed:		
Currency Pair	Buy / Sell	Trade Size	Entry Price	Target Price	Stop Loss	Closing Price
Profit /Loss (Pips):		Strategy:		Notes:		

Date:		Time Open:		Time Closed:		
Currency Pair	Buy / Sell	Trade Size	Entry Price	Target Price	Stop Loss	Closing Price
Profit /Loss (Pips):		Strategy:		Notes:		

Date:		Time Open:		Time Closed:		
Currency Pair	Buy / Sell	Trade Size	Entry Price	Target Price	Stop Loss	Closing Price
Profit /Loss (Pips):		Strategy:		Notes:		

Date:		Time Open:		Time Closed:		
Currency Pair	Buy / Sell	Trade Size	Entry Price	Target Price	Stop Loss	Closing Price
Profit /Loss (Pips):		Strategy:		Notes:		

Date:		Time Open:		Time Closed:		
Currency Pair	Buy / Sell	Trade Size	Entry Price	Target Price	Stop Loss	Closing Price
Profit /Loss (Pips):		Strategy:		Notes:		

Date:		Time Open:		Time Closed:		
Currency Pair	Buy / Sell	Trade Size	Entry Price	Target Price	Stop Loss	Closing Price
Profit /Loss (Pips):		Strategy:		Notes:		

Date:		Time Open:		Time Closed:		
Currency Pair	Buy / Sell	Trade Size	Entry Price	Target Price	Stop Loss	Closing Price
Profit /Loss (Pips):		Strategy:		Notes:		

Date:		Time Open:		Time Closed:		
Currency Pair	Buy / Sell	Trade Size	Entry Price	Target Price	Stop Loss	Closing Price
Profit /Loss (Pips):		Strategy:		Notes:		

Date:		Time Open:		Time Closed:		
Currency Pair	Buy / Sell	Trade Size	Entry Price	Target Price	Stop Loss	Closing Price
Profit /Loss (Pips):		Strategy:		Notes:		

Date:		Time Open:		Time Closed:		
Currency Pair	Buy / Sell	Trade Size	Entry Price	Target Price	Stop Loss	Closing Price
Profit /Loss (Pips):		Strategy:		Notes:		

Date:		Time Open:		Time Closed:		
Currency Pair	Buy / Sell	Trade Size	Entry Price	Target Price	Stop Loss	Closing Price
Profit /Loss (Pips):		Strategy:		Notes:		

Date:		Time Open:		Time Closed:		
Currency Pair	Buy / Sell	Trade Size	Entry Price	Target Price	Stop Loss	Closing Price
Profit /Loss (Pips):		Strategy:		Notes:		

Date:		Time Open:		Time Closed:		
Currency Pair	Buy / Sell	Trade Size	Entry Price	Target Price	Stop Loss	Closing Price
Profit /Loss (Pips):		Strategy:		Notes:		

Date:		Time Open:		Time Closed:		
Currency Pair	Buy / Sell	Trade Size	Entry Price	Target Price	Stop Loss	Closing Price
Profit /Loss (Pips):		Strategy:		Notes:		

Date:		Time Open:		Time Closed:		
Currency Pair	Buy / Sell	Trade Size	Entry Price	Target Price	Stop Loss	Closing Price
Profit /Loss (Pips):		Strategy:		Notes:		

Date:		Time Open:		Time Closed:		
Currency Pair	Buy / Sell	Trade Size	Entry Price	Target Price	Stop Loss	Closing Price
Profit /Loss (Pips):		Strategy:		Notes:		

Date:		Time Open:		Time Closed:		
Currency Pair	Buy / Sell	Trade Size	Entry Price	Target Price	Stop Loss	Closing Price
Profit /Loss (Pips):		Strategy:		Notes:		

Date:		Time Open:		Time Closed:		
Currency Pair	Buy / Sell	Trade Size	Entry Price	Target Price	Stop Loss	Closing Price
Profit /Loss (Pips):		Strategy:		Notes:		

Date:		Time Open:		Time Closed:		
Currency Pair	Buy / Sell	Trade Size	Entry Price	Target Price	Stop Loss	Closing Price
Profit /Loss (Pips):		Strategy:		Notes:		

Date:		Time Open:		Time Closed:		
Currency Pair	Buy / Sell	Trade Size	Entry Price	Target Price	Stop Loss	Closing Price
Profit /Loss (Pips):		Strategy:		Notes:		

Date:		Time Open:		Time Closed:		
Currency Pair	**Buy / Sell**	**Trade Size**	**Entry Price**	**Target Price**	**Stop Loss**	**Closing Price**
Profit /Loss (Pips):		**Strategy:**		**Notes:**		

Date:		Time Open:		Time Closed:		
Currency Pair	**Buy / Sell**	**Trade Size**	**Entry Price**	**Target Price**	**Stop Loss**	**Closing Price**
Profit /Loss (Pips):		**Strategy:**		**Notes:**		

Date:		Time Open:		Time Closed:		
Currency Pair	**Buy / Sell**	**Trade Size**	**Entry Price**	**Target Price**	**Stop Loss**	**Closing Price**
Profit /Loss (Pips):		**Strategy:**		**Notes:**		

Date:		Time Open:		Time Closed:		
Currency Pair	**Buy / Sell**	**Trade Size**	**Entry Price**	**Target Price**	**Stop Loss**	**Closing Price**
Profit /Loss (Pips):		**Strategy:**		**Notes:**		

Date:		Time Open:		Time Closed:		
Currency Pair	**Buy / Sell**	**Trade Size**	**Entry Price**	**Target Price**	**Stop Loss**	**Closing Price**
Profit /Loss (Pips):		**Strategy:**		**Notes:**		

Date:		Time Open:		Time Closed:		
Currency Pair	Buy / Sell	Trade Size	Entry Price	Target Price	Stop Loss	Closing Price
Profit /Loss (Pips):		Strategy:		Notes:		

Date:		Time Open:		Time Closed:		
Currency Pair	Buy / Sell	Trade Size	Entry Price	Target Price	Stop Loss	Closing Price
Profit /Loss (Pips):		Strategy:		Notes:		

Date:		Time Open:		Time Closed:		
Currency Pair	Buy / Sell	Trade Size	Entry Price	Target Price	Stop Loss	Closing Price
Profit /Loss (Pips):		Strategy:		Notes:		

Date:		Time Open:		Time Closed:		
Currency Pair	Buy / Sell	Trade Size	Entry Price	Target Price	Stop Loss	Closing Price
Profit /Loss (Pips):		Strategy:		Notes:		

Date:		Time Open:		Time Closed:		
Currency Pair	Buy / Sell	Trade Size	Entry Price	Target Price	Stop Loss	Closing Price
Profit /Loss (Pips):		Strategy:		Notes:		

Date:		Time Open:		Time Closed:		
Currency Pair	Buy / Sell	Trade Size	Entry Price	Target Price	Stop Loss	Closing Price
Profit /Loss (Pips):		Strategy:		Notes:		

Date:		Time Open:		Time Closed:		
Currency Pair	Buy / Sell	Trade Size	Entry Price	Target Price	Stop Loss	Closing Price
Profit /Loss (Pips):		Strategy:		Notes:		

Date:		Time Open:		Time Closed:		
Currency Pair	Buy / Sell	Trade Size	Entry Price	Target Price	Stop Loss	Closing Price
Profit /Loss (Pips):		Strategy:		Notes:		

Date:		Time Open:		Time Closed:		
Currency Pair	Buy / Sell	Trade Size	Entry Price	Target Price	Stop Loss	Closing Price
Profit /Loss (Pips):		Strategy:		Notes:		

Date:		Time Open:		Time Closed:		
Currency Pair	Buy / Sell	Trade Size	Entry Price	Target Price	Stop Loss	Closing Price
Profit /Loss (Pips):		Strategy:		Notes:		

Date:		Time Open:		Time Closed:		
Currency Pair	Buy / Sell	Trade Size	Entry Price	Target Price	Stop Loss	Closing Price
Profit /Loss (Pips):		Strategy:		Notes:		

Date:		Time Open:		Time Closed:		
Currency Pair	Buy / Sell	Trade Size	Entry Price	Target Price	Stop Loss	Closing Price
Profit /Loss (Pips):		Strategy:		Notes:		

Date:		Time Open:		Time Closed:		
Currency Pair	Buy / Sell	Trade Size	Entry Price	Target Price	Stop Loss	Closing Price
Profit /Loss (Pips):		Strategy:		Notes:		

Date:		Time Open:		Time Closed:		
Currency Pair	Buy / Sell	Trade Size	Entry Price	Target Price	Stop Loss	Closing Price
Profit /Loss (Pips):		Strategy:		Notes:		

Date:		Time Open:		Time Closed:		
Currency Pair	Buy / Sell	Trade Size	Entry Price	Target Price	Stop Loss	Closing Price
Profit /Loss (Pips):		Strategy:		Notes:		

Date:		Time Open:		Time Closed:		
Currency Pair	Buy / Sell	Trade Size	Entry Price	Target Price	Stop Loss	Closing Price
Profit /Loss (Pips):		Strategy:		Notes:		

Date:		Time Open:		Time Closed:		
Currency Pair	Buy / Sell	Trade Size	Entry Price	Target Price	Stop Loss	Closing Price
Profit /Loss (Pips):		Strategy:		Notes:		

Date:		Time Open:		Time Closed:		
Currency Pair	Buy / Sell	Trade Size	Entry Price	Target Price	Stop Loss	Closing Price
Profit /Loss (Pips):		Strategy:		Notes:		

Date:		Time Open:		Time Closed:		
Currency Pair	Buy / Sell	Trade Size	Entry Price	Target Price	Stop Loss	Closing Price
Profit /Loss (Pips):		Strategy:		Notes:		

Date:		Time Open:		Time Closed:		
Currency Pair	Buy / Sell	Trade Size	Entry Price	Target Price	Stop Loss	Closing Price
Profit /Loss (Pips):		Strategy:		Notes:		

Date:		Time Open:		Time Closed:		
Currency Pair	Buy / Sell	Trade Size	Entry Price	Target Price	Stop Loss	Closing Price
Profit /Loss (Pips):		Strategy:		Notes:		

Date:		Time Open:		Time Closed:		
Currency Pair	Buy / Sell	Trade Size	Entry Price	Target Price	Stop Loss	Closing Price
Profit /Loss (Pips):		Strategy:		Notes:		

Date:		Time Open:		Time Closed:		
Currency Pair	Buy / Sell	Trade Size	Entry Price	Target Price	Stop Loss	Closing Price
Profit /Loss (Pips):		Strategy:		Notes:		

Date:		Time Open:		Time Closed:		
Currency Pair	Buy / Sell	Trade Size	Entry Price	Target Price	Stop Loss	Closing Price
Profit /Loss (Pips):		Strategy:		Notes:		

Date:		Time Open:		Time Closed:		
Currency Pair	Buy / Sell	Trade Size	Entry Price	Target Price	Stop Loss	Closing Price
Profit /Loss (Pips):		Strategy:		Notes:		

Date:		Time Open:		Time Closed:		
Currency Pair	**Buy / Sell**	**Trade Size**	**Entry Price**	**Target Price**	**Stop Loss**	**Closing Price**
Profit /Loss (Pips):		Strategy:		Notes:		

Date:		Time Open:		Time Closed:		
Currency Pair	**Buy / Sell**	**Trade Size**	**Entry Price**	**Target Price**	**Stop Loss**	**Closing Price**
Profit /Loss (Pips):		Strategy:		Notes:		

Date:		Time Open:		Time Closed:		
Currency Pair	**Buy / Sell**	**Trade Size**	**Entry Price**	**Target Price**	**Stop Loss**	**Closing Price**
Profit /Loss (Pips):		Strategy:		Notes:		

Date:		Time Open:		Time Closed:		
Currency Pair	**Buy / Sell**	**Trade Size**	**Entry Price**	**Target Price**	**Stop Loss**	**Closing Price**
Profit /Loss (Pips):		Strategy:		Notes:		

Date:		Time Open:		Time Closed:		
Currency Pair	**Buy / Sell**	**Trade Size**	**Entry Price**	**Target Price**	**Stop Loss**	**Closing Price**
Profit /Loss (Pips):		Strategy:		Notes:		

Date:		Time Open:		Time Closed:		
Currency Pair	Buy / Sell	Trade Size	Entry Price	Target Price	Stop Loss	Closing Price
Profit /Loss (Pips):		Strategy:		Notes:		

Date:		Time Open:		Time Closed:		
Currency Pair	Buy / Sell	Trade Size	Entry Price	Target Price	Stop Loss	Closing Price
Profit /Loss (Pips):		Strategy:		Notes:		

Date:		Time Open:		Time Closed:		
Currency Pair	Buy / Sell	Trade Size	Entry Price	Target Price	Stop Loss	Closing Price
Profit /Loss (Pips):		Strategy:		Notes:		

Date:		Time Open:		Time Closed:		
Currency Pair	Buy / Sell	Trade Size	Entry Price	Target Price	Stop Loss	Closing Price
Profit /Loss (Pips):		Strategy:		Notes:		

Date:		Time Open:		Time Closed:		
Currency Pair	Buy / Sell	Trade Size	Entry Price	Target Price	Stop Loss	Closing Price
Profit /Loss (Pips):		Strategy:		Notes:		

Date:		Time Open:		Time Closed:		
Currency Pair	Buy / Sell	Trade Size	Entry Price	Target Price	Stop Loss	Closing Price
Profit /Loss (Pips):		Strategy:		Notes:		

Date:		Time Open:		Time Closed:		
Currency Pair	Buy / Sell	Trade Size	Entry Price	Target Price	Stop Loss	Closing Price
Profit /Loss (Pips):		Strategy:		Notes:		

Date:		Time Open:		Time Closed:		
Currency Pair	Buy / Sell	Trade Size	Entry Price	Target Price	Stop Loss	Closing Price
Profit /Loss (Pips):		Strategy:		Notes:		

Date:		Time Open:		Time Closed:		
Currency Pair	Buy / Sell	Trade Size	Entry Price	Target Price	Stop Loss	Closing Price
Profit /Loss (Pips):		Strategy:		Notes:		

Date:		Time Open:		Time Closed:		
Currency Pair	Buy / Sell	Trade Size	Entry Price	Target Price	Stop Loss	Closing Price
Profit /Loss (Pips):		Strategy:		Notes:		

Date:		Time Open:		Time Closed:		
Currency Pair	Buy / Sell	Trade Size	Entry Price	Target Price	Stop Loss	Closing Price
Profit /Loss (Pips):		Strategy:		Notes:		

Date:		Time Open:		Time Closed:		
Currency Pair	Buy / Sell	Trade Size	Entry Price	Target Price	Stop Loss	Closing Price
Profit /Loss (Pips):		Strategy:		Notes:		

Date:		Time Open:		Time Closed:		
Currency Pair	Buy / Sell	Trade Size	Entry Price	Target Price	Stop Loss	Closing Price
Profit /Loss (Pips):		Strategy:		Notes:		

Date:		Time Open:		Time Closed:		
Currency Pair	Buy / Sell	Trade Size	Entry Price	Target Price	Stop Loss	Closing Price
Profit /Loss (Pips):		Strategy:		Notes:		

Date:		Time Open:		Time Closed:		
Currency Pair	Buy / Sell	Trade Size	Entry Price	Target Price	Stop Loss	Closing Price
Profit /Loss (Pips):		Strategy:		Notes:		

Date:		Time Open:		Time Closed:		
Currency Pair	Buy / Sell	Trade Size	Entry Price	Target Price	Stop Loss	Closing Price
Profit /Loss (Pips):		Strategy:		Notes:		

Date:		Time Open:		Time Closed:		
Currency Pair	Buy / Sell	Trade Size	Entry Price	Target Price	Stop Loss	Closing Price
Profit /Loss (Pips):		Strategy:		Notes:		

Date:		Time Open:		Time Closed:		
Currency Pair	Buy / Sell	Trade Size	Entry Price	Target Price	Stop Loss	Closing Price
Profit /Loss (Pips):		Strategy:		Notes:		

Date:		Time Open:		Time Closed:		
Currency Pair	Buy / Sell	Trade Size	Entry Price	Target Price	Stop Loss	Closing Price
Profit /Loss (Pips):		Strategy:		Notes:		

Date:		Time Open:		Time Closed:		
Currency Pair	Buy / Sell	Trade Size	Entry Price	Target Price	Stop Loss	Closing Price
Profit /Loss (Pips):		Strategy:		Notes:		

Date:		Time Open:		Time Closed:		
Currency Pair	Buy / Sell	Trade Size	Entry Price	Target Price	Stop Loss	Closing Price
Profit /Loss (Pips):		Strategy:		Notes:		

Date:		Time Open:		Time Closed:		
Currency Pair	Buy / Sell	Trade Size	Entry Price	Target Price	Stop Loss	Closing Price
Profit /Loss (Pips):		Strategy:		Notes:		

Date:		Time Open:		Time Closed:		
Currency Pair	Buy / Sell	Trade Size	Entry Price	Target Price	Stop Loss	Closing Price
Profit /Loss (Pips):		Strategy:		Notes:		

Date:		Time Open:		Time Closed:		
Currency Pair	Buy / Sell	Trade Size	Entry Price	Target Price	Stop Loss	Closing Price
Profit /Loss (Pips):		Strategy:		Notes:		

Date:		Time Open:		Time Closed:		
Currency Pair	Buy / Sell	Trade Size	Entry Price	Target Price	Stop Loss	Closing Price
Profit /Loss (Pips):		Strategy:		Notes:		

Date:		Time Open:		Time Closed:		
Currency Pair	Buy / Sell	Trade Size	Entry Price	Target Price	Stop Loss	Closing Price
Profit /Loss (Pips):		Strategy:		Notes:		

Date:		Time Open:		Time Closed:		
Currency Pair	Buy / Sell	Trade Size	Entry Price	Target Price	Stop Loss	Closing Price
Profit /Loss (Pips):		Strategy:		Notes:		

Date:		Time Open:		Time Closed:		
Currency Pair	Buy / Sell	Trade Size	Entry Price	Target Price	Stop Loss	Closing Price
Profit /Loss (Pips):		Strategy:		Notes:		

Date:		Time Open:		Time Closed:		
Currency Pair	Buy / Sell	Trade Size	Entry Price	Target Price	Stop Loss	Closing Price
Profit /Loss (Pips):		Strategy:		Notes:		

Date:		Time Open:		Time Closed:		
Currency Pair	Buy / Sell	Trade Size	Entry Price	Target Price	Stop Loss	Closing Price
Profit /Loss (Pips):		Strategy:		Notes:		

MY
FOREX TRADING
STRATEGIES

Trading Strategy Name:	**Currency Pair:**

Indicators Used	
Buy Signal	
Sell Signal	
Profit Target	
Stop Loss	
Notes	

Trading Strategy Name:		Currency Pair:
Indicators Used		
Buy Signal		
Sell Signal		
Profit Target		
Stop Loss		
Notes		

Trading Strategy Name:	Currency Pair:
Indicators Used	
Buy Signal	
Sell Signal	
Profit Target	
Stop Loss	
Notes	

Trading Strategy Name:		Currency Pair:
Indicators Used		
Buy Signal		
Sell Signal		
Profit Target		
Stop Loss		
Notes		

Trading Strategy Name:	Currency Pair:

Indicators Used	
Buy Signal	
Sell Signal	
Profit Target	
Stop Loss	
Notes	

Trading Strategy Name:	Currency Pair:

Indicators Used	
Buy Signal	
Sell Signal	
Profit Target	
Stop Loss	
Notes	

Trading Strategy Name:	Currency Pair:
Indicators Used	
Buy Signal	
Sell Signal	
Profit Target	
Stop Loss	
Notes	

Trading Strategy Name:	**Currency Pair:**

Indicators Used	
Buy Signal	
Sell Signal	
Profit Target	
Stop Loss	
Notes	

Trading Strategy Name:	Currency Pair:

Indicators Used	
Buy Signal	
Sell Signal	
Profit Target	
Stop Loss	
Notes	

Trading Strategy Name:		Currency Pair:
Indicators Used		
Buy Signal		
Sell Signal		
Profit Target		
Stop Loss		
Notes		

Trading Strategy Name:	Currency Pair:
Indicators Used	
Buy Signal	
Sell Signal	
Profit Target	
Stop Loss	
Notes	

Trading Strategy Name:		**Currency Pair:**
Indicators Used		
Buy Signal		
Sell Signal		
Profit Target		
Stop Loss		
Notes		

Trading Strategy Name:		Currency Pair:
Indicators Used		
Buy Signal		
Sell Signal		
Profit Target		
Stop Loss		
Notes		

Trading Strategy Name:	Currency Pair:

Indicators Used	
Buy Signal	
Sell Signal	
Profit Target	
Stop Loss	
Notes	

Trading Strategy Name:		Currency Pair:
Indicators Used		
Buy Signal		
Sell Signal		
Profit Target		
Stop Loss		
Notes		

Trading Strategy Name:		Currency Pair:
Indicators Used		
Buy Signal		
Sell Signal		
Profit Target		
Stop Loss		
Notes		

Trading Strategy Name:	Currency Pair:

Indicators Used	
Buy Signal	
Sell Signal	
Profit Target	
Stop Loss	
Notes	

Trading Strategy Name:	Currency Pair:
Indicators Used	
Buy Signal	
Sell Signal	
Profit Target	
Stop Loss	
Notes	

Trading Strategy Name:	Currency Pair:

Indicators Used	
Buy Signal	
Sell Signal	
Profit Target	
Stop Loss	
Notes	

Trading Strategy Name:		Currency Pair:
Indicators Used		
Buy Signal		
Sell Signal		
Profit Target		
Stop Loss		
Notes		

Trading Strategy Name:		Currency Pair:
Indicators Used		
Buy Signal		
Sell Signal		
Profit Target		
Stop Loss		
Notes		

	Trading Strategy Name:	Currency Pair:
Indicators Used		
Buy Signal		
Sell Signal		
Profit Target		
Stop Loss		
Notes		

Trading Strategy Name:	Currency Pair:

Indicators Used	
Buy Signal	
Sell Signal	
Profit Target	
Stop Loss	
Notes	

Trading Strategy Name:	**Currency Pair:**
Indicators Used	
Buy Signal	
Sell Signal	
Profit Target	
Stop Loss	
Notes	

Trading Strategy Name:	Currency Pair:

Indicators Used	
Buy Signal	
Sell Signal	
Profit Target	
Stop Loss	
Notes	

Trading Strategy Name:	**Currency Pair:**

Indicators Used	
Buy Signal	
Sell Signal	
Profit Target	
Stop Loss	
Notes	

Trading Strategy Name:	**Currency Pair:**

Indicators Used	
Buy Signal	
Sell Signal	
Profit Target	
Stop Loss	
Notes	

Trading Strategy Name:	Currency Pair:
Indicators Used	
Buy Signal	
Sell Signal	
Profit Target	
Stop Loss	
Notes	

Trading Strategy Name:	Currency Pair:

Indicators Used	
Buy Signal	
Sell Signal	
Profit Target	
Stop Loss	
Notes	

Trading Strategy Name:		Currency Pair:
Indicators Used		
Buy Signal		
Sell Signal		
Profit Target		
Stop Loss		
Notes		

Trading Strategy Name:	Currency Pair:
Indicators Used	
Buy Signal	
Sell Signal	
Profit Target	
Stop Loss	
Notes	

Trading Strategy Name:	Currency Pair:

Indicators Used	
Buy Signal	
Sell Signal	
Profit Target	
Stop Loss	
Notes	

Trading Strategy Name:	Currency Pair:

Indicators Used	
Buy Signal	
Sell Signal	
Profit Target	
Stop Loss	
Notes	

Trading Strategy Name:		Currency Pair:

Indicators Used	
Buy Signal	
Sell Signal	
Profit Target	
Stop Loss	
Notes	

Trading Strategy Name:	**Currency Pair:**

Indicators Used	
Buy Signal	
Sell Signal	
Profit Target	
Stop Loss	
Notes	

Trading Strategy Name:	**Currency Pair:**

Indicators Used	
Buy Signal	
Sell Signal	
Profit Target	
Stop Loss	
Notes	

Trading Strategy Name:	Currency Pair:

Indicators Used	
Buy Signal	
Sell Signal	
Profit Target	
Stop Loss	
Notes	

Trading Strategy Name:		Currency Pair:
Indicators Used		
Buy Signal		
Sell Signal		
Profit Target		
Stop Loss		
Notes		

Trading Strategy Name:	**Currency Pair:**

Indicators Used	
Buy Signal	
Sell Signal	
Profit Target	
Stop Loss	
Notes	

Trading Strategy Name:	Currency Pair:
Indicators Used	
Buy Signal	
Sell Signal	
Profit Target	
Stop Loss	
Notes	

Trading Strategy Name:	Currency Pair:

Indicators Used	
Buy Signal	
Sell Signal	
Profit Target	
Stop Loss	
Notes	

Trading Strategy Name:		Currency Pair:
Indicators Used		
Buy Signal		
Sell Signal		
Profit Target		
Stop Loss STOP		
Notes		

Trading Strategy Name:	**Currency Pair:**

Indicators Used	
Buy Signal	
Sell Signal	
Profit Target	
Stop Loss	
Notes	

	Trading Strategy Name:	Currency Pair:
Indicators Used		
Buy Signal		
Sell Signal		
Profit Target		
Stop Loss		
Notes		

Trading Strategy Name:	Currency Pair:

Indicators Used	
Buy Signal	
Sell Signal	
Profit Target	
Stop Loss	
Notes	

	Trading Strategy Name:	Currency Pair:
Indicators Used		
Buy Signal		
Sell Signal		
Profit Target		
Stop Loss		
Notes		

Trading Strategy Name:	Currency Pair:

Indicators Used	
Buy Signal	
Sell Signal	
Profit Target	
Stop Loss	
Notes	

Trading Strategy Name:	**Currency Pair:**

Indicators Used	
Buy Signal	
Sell Signal	
Profit Target	
Stop Loss	
Notes	

Trading Strategy Name:	**Currency Pair:**

Indicators Used	
Buy Signal	
Sell Signal	
Profit Target	
Stop Loss	
Notes	

Trading Strategy Name:		Currency Pair:
Indicators Used		
Buy Signal		
Sell Signal		
Profit Target		
Stop Loss		
Notes		

Trading Strategy Name:	Currency Pair:

Indicators Used	
Buy Signal	
Sell Signal	
Profit Target	
Stop Loss	
Notes	

INDEX

	Page

INDEX	
	Page

INDEX	
	Page

INDEX	
	Page

INDEX	
	Page

INDEX	Page

INDEX	
	Page

INDEX

	Page

INDEX

	Page